Book Title:

"Effortless Frugality: 25 Tips to Save Money and Maximize Efficiency"

Frugal Living and Productivity Tips: Volume 1

By Jenny Koo

Imprint: Independently published.

Copyright © 2024 by Jenny K. Koo. All rights reserved.

No part of this book may be used or reproduced in any manner whatsoever without written permission.

For information, please email to
jennykookk@gmail.com

Table of Contents

Introduction
- The Importance of Frugal Living
- How This Book Can Help You Save Money and Resources
- An Overview of What You'll Learn

Chapter 1: Upcycling and Repurposing
1. Tip #1
2. Tip #2
3. Tip #3
4. Tip #4
5. Tip #5

Chapter 2: Eco-Friendly Practices
1. Tip #1
2. Tip #2
3. Tip #3
4. Tip #4
5. Tip #5

Chapter 3: Home and Garden Hacks
1. Tip #1
2. Tip #2
3. Tip #3
4. Tip #4
5. Tip #5

Chapter 4: DIY Projects and Homemade Solutions

1. Tip #1
2. Tip #2
3. Tip #3
4. Tip #4
5. Tip #5

Chapter 5: Thrifty Shopping and Resource Management

1. Tip #1
2. Tip #2
3. Tip #3
4. Tip #4
5. Tip #5

Conclusion

- Recap of Key Points
- Encouragement to Adopt Frugal and Productive Habits
- Teaser for Volume 2
- Invitation for Reader Feedback

Appendix

- Additional Resources
    - Books, Websites, and Tools for Further Reading and Exploration
- Worksheets and Templates
    - Budget Templates, DIY Project Plans, and Frugality Trackers

Introduction

The Importance of Frugal Living

In today's fast-paced world, where consumerism often overshadows practicality, frugal living is a beacon of simplicity and efficiency. Adopting a frugal lifestyle doesn't mean compromising on quality or comfort; rather, it emphasizes making smart, sustainable choices that enhance our lives and reduce waste. By embracing frugality, you can save money, time, and resources while contributing to a healthier planet.

How This Book Can Help You Save Money and Resources

This book is designed to be a practical guide for anyone looking to incorporate frugal living into their daily routine. Whether you're a young professional, a busy parent, a college student, or a retiree, the tips and strategies provided here are tailored to fit various lifestyles and needs. From repurposing household items to eco-friendly practices and money-saving hacks, you'll find actionable advice that you can start implementing immediately.

An Overview of What You'll Learn

In this first volume, we will explore 25 practical tips for frugal living. Each chapter is dedicated to a specific aspect of frugality, providing detailed instructions, real-life examples, and practical advice on how to implement these tips in your daily life. By the end of this book, you'll be equipped with the knowledge and inspiration to make frugality a natural and rewarding part of your everyday routine.

Chapter 1: Upcycling and Repurposing

Tip 1: Make Homemade Cleaning Cloths from Old T-Shirts

Introduction

Why This Tip Matters: Switching to homemade cleaning cloths not only saves money but also helps reduce waste. Old t-shirts that would otherwise be thrown away can find a new purpose, making this a frugal and environmentally friendly choice.

In-Depth Information

How to Make Homemade Cleaning Cloths:

1. **Materials Needed:**
    - Old t-shirts
    - Scissors
    - Ruler (optional for measuring)
2. **Steps:**
    - Lay the t-shirt flat and smooth out any wrinkles.
    - Use scissors to cut the t-shirt into squares or rectangles of your desired size. Common sizes are 12x12 inches or 6x6 inches, but you can adjust based on your needs.
    - You can leave the edges raw or hem them if you prefer a neater finish. Hemming will help prevent fraying, but it's not necessary for most cleaning tasks.

Real-Life Example

Example: Sarah, a busy mother of two, used this tip to create a set of 20 cleaning cloths from her family's old t-shirts. Not only did she save money on paper towels, but she also found that the cloths were more durable and effective for cleaning up spills and dusting surfaces.

Implementation in Daily Life

How to Use Homemade Cleaning Cloths:

- **For Dusting:** These cloths are great for dusting furniture, blinds, and electronics. They can be used dry or slightly dampened.
- **For Spills:** Keep a few cloths in the kitchen for quick clean-ups of spills and messes.
- **For Windows:** Pair these cloths with a homemade vinegar solution for streak-free window cleaning.

Maintenance Tips:

- Wash the cloths regularly to keep them hygienic. You can wash them with your regular laundry.
- Designate specific cloths for different tasks (e.g., one set for the kitchen, another for the bathroom) to avoid cross-contamination.

Tip 2: Turn Old Sheets into Curtains

Introduction

Why This Tip Matters: Repurposing old sheets into curtains is an excellent way to save money on home decor while reducing waste. This simple DIY project can add a personal touch to your living space and help you control indoor temperatures more effectively.

In-Depth Information

How to Turn Old Sheets into Curtains:

1. **Materials Needed:**
    - Old sheets
    - Scissors
    - Sewing machine or fabric glue
    - Curtain rod and hooks
2. **Steps:**
    - Measure the window and cut the sheets to the appropriate size, allowing extra fabric for hems and loops.
    - Hem the edges for a neat finish. If you don't have a sewing machine, fabric glue works as a quick alternative.
    - Create loops or a pocket at the top for the curtain rod. This can be done by folding the top edge over and sewing or gluing it in place.
    - Hang the curtains on the rod and adjust as needed.

Real-Life Example

Example: John, an avid DIY enthusiast, transformed his old bed sheets into stylish living room curtains. He saved money on new curtains and was able to match the colors perfectly with his existing decor.

Implementation in Daily Life

How to Use Sheet Curtains:

- **For Bedrooms:** Use heavier sheets for blackout curtains to improve sleep quality.
- **For Living Areas:** Lighter sheets can be used to create airy, sunlit spaces while still providing privacy.
- **Seasonal Changes:** Switch out sheet curtains seasonally for a fresh look and improved energy efficiency.

Maintenance Tips:

- Wash the curtains regularly to keep them clean and fresh.
- If you used fabric glue, avoid machine washing and opt for gentle hand washing instead.

Tip 3: Turn Old Jeans into Shorts
Introduction
Why This Tip Matters: Transforming old jeans into shorts is a practical way to extend the life of your clothing. This simple upcycling project is perfect for creating custom summer wear without spending extra money.

In-Depth Information
How to Turn Old Jeans into Shorts:

1. **Materials Needed:**
    - Old jeans
    - Scissors
    - Chalk or fabric marker
    - Sewing machine or needle and thread (optional)
2. **Steps:**

- Put on the jeans and mark the desired length with chalk or a fabric marker.
- Lay the jeans flat and cut across the mark. Cut slightly longer than the desired length to allow for adjustments.
- Try on the shorts and make any necessary adjustments to the length. You can roll up the hems for a casual look or hem them for a cleaner finish.

Real-Life Example

Example: Emily, a college student on a budget, repurposed her old jeans into a stylish pair of summer shorts. She enjoyed the process and appreciated the savings, allowing her to allocate more money towards her studies.

Implementation in Daily Life
How to Style and Use DIY Shorts:

- **Casual Wear:** Pair the shorts with t-shirts or tank tops for a relaxed, everyday look.
- **Beach Outfits:** Use the shorts as part of your beach attire, easy to slip on over swimwear.
- **Layering:** Wear the shorts with leggings or tights during cooler weather for a versatile, layered outfit.

Maintenance Tips:

- Wash the shorts as you would your regular jeans.
- If the hems start to fray, trim the edges or re-hem them to maintain the desired look.

Tip 4: Create a Braided Rug from Old Clothes

Introduction

Why This Tip Matters: Creating a braided rug from old clothes is a fantastic way to recycle fabric and add a unique, handmade touch to your home decor. This project helps reduce textile waste and provides a durable, stylish rug for any room.

In-Depth Information

How to Create a Braided Rug:

1. **Materials Needed:**
   - Old clothes (t-shirts, sheets, etc.)
   - Scissors
   - Needle and thread or fabric glue
2. **Steps:**
   - Cut the old clothes into long strips, approximately 1-2 inches wide.
   - Braid the strips together, adding more strips as needed to create a long braid.
   - Coil the braid into a spiral, stitching or gluing the coils together as you go.
   - Continue adding to the braid and coiling until the rug reaches the desired size.

Real-Life Example

Example: Karen, a retiree looking for a new hobby, created a beautiful braided rug from her old clothes. Not only did she enjoy the creative process, but she also produced a durable rug that added charm to her living room.

Implementation in Daily Life

How to Use Braided Rugs:

- **Entryways:** Place the rug in your entryway to catch dirt and debris from shoes.
- **Living Spaces:** Use the rug to add warmth and texture to your living room or bedroom.
- **Outdoor Areas:** Create a weather-resistant version using old synthetic fabrics for use on patios or balconies.

Maintenance Tips:

- Vacuum the rug regularly to keep it clean.
- Spot clean with mild soap and water as needed.
- If the rug becomes heavily soiled, gently hand wash it and allow it to air dry.

Tip 5: Use Old Jars for Food Storage

Introduction

Why This Tip Matters: Repurposing old jars for food storage is an eco-friendly and cost-effective way to organize your kitchen. Glass jars are durable, reusable, and help reduce plastic waste.

In-Depth Information

How to Use Old Jars for Food Storage:

1. **Materials Needed:**
    - Old jars (with lids)
    - Labels (optional)
2. **Steps:**
    - Clean and sterilize the jars by washing them with hot, soapy water and allowing them to air dry.

- Use the jars to store dry goods such as rice, pasta, beans, and spices.
- Label the jars for easy identification. You can use adhesive labels or write directly on the jars with a permanent marker.

Real-Life Example

Example: Mark, a single professional, repurposed his old pasta sauce jars for pantry organization. He found that using jars not only saved him money but also made his pantry more visually appealing and easier to navigate.

Implementation in Daily Life

How to Utilize Jars:

- **Pantry Organization:** Store bulk items like grains, nuts, and seeds in jars to keep them fresh and organized.
- **Refrigerator Storage:** Use jars for leftovers, homemade sauces, and pickles.
- **Meal Prep:** Prepare and store individual portions of salads, overnight oats, and smoothies in jars for quick, grab-and-go meals.

Maintenance Tips:

- Wash jars thoroughly after each use to prevent contamination.
- Check the lids regularly to ensure they seal properly.
- Replace any jars that develop cracks or chips to avoid potential hazards.

Chapter 2: Eco-Friendly Practices

Tip 1: Use a Reusable Razor

Introduction

Why This Tip Matters: Switching to a reusable razor is a simple yet effective way to reduce plastic waste and save money in the long run. Disposable razors contribute significantly to landfill waste, while reusable razors are more durable and cost-efficient over time.

In-Depth Information

How to Use a Reusable Razor:

1. **Types of Reusable Razors:**
   - Safety razors
   - Straight razors
   - Electric razors
2. **Steps for Using a Safety Razor:**
   - Choose a quality safety razor with replaceable blades.
   - Wet your skin and apply shaving cream or soap.
   - Shave in the direction of hair growth, using short, gentle strokes.
   - Rinse the razor frequently during use.
   - After shaving, rinse the razor thoroughly and allow it to dry completely.

Real-Life Example

Example: Tom, an eco-conscious professional, switched to a safety razor to reduce his plastic footprint. He found that not only did he save money on disposable razors, but he also enjoyed a closer, smoother shave.

Implementation in Daily Life
How to Integrate Reusable Razors:

- **Daily Shaving Routine:** Incorporate the reusable razor into your regular grooming routine.
- **Travel:** Invest in a travel case for your razor to maintain your eco-friendly habits on the go.
- **Maintenance:** Replace the blades as needed and clean the razor regularly to ensure longevity.

Maintenance Tips:

- Dry the razor completely after each use to prevent rusting.
- Store the razor in a dry place.
- Replace blades when they become dull to maintain effective shaving.

Tip 2: Use Reusable Menstrual Products
Introduction

Why This Tip Matters: Reusable menstrual products, such as menstrual cups, cloth pads, and period underwear, offer a sustainable and cost-effective alternative to disposable products. These options reduce waste and are often more comfortable and convenient.

In-Depth Information
Types of Reusable Menstrual Products:

1. **Menstrual Cups:**
    - Made of medical-grade silicone or rubber.

- Inserted into the vagina to collect menstrual fluid.
2. **Cloth Pads:**
    - Made of absorbent fabric.
    - Used like disposable pads but washed and reused.
3. **Period Underwear:**
    - Built-in absorbent layers.
    - Worn like regular underwear.

Real-Life Example

Example: Lisa, a college student, switched to using a menstrual cup and cloth pads. She appreciated the cost savings and found them more comfortable than disposable products. Plus, she felt good about reducing her environmental impact.

Implementation in Daily Life

How to Use Reusable Menstrual Products:

- **Menstrual Cups:** Insert and remove according to instructions. Empty, rinse, and reinsert as needed.
- **Cloth Pads:** Change as often as needed, wash thoroughly, and air dry.
- **Period Underwear:** Wear on lighter days or as backup. Wash and dry according to the manufacturer's instructions.

Maintenance Tips:

- Sterilize menstrual cups between cycles.
- Wash cloth pads and period underwear with gentle, fragrance-free detergent.
- Store in a clean, dry place.

Tip 3: Use Reusable Food Wraps Instead of Plastic

Introduction

Why This Tip Matters: Reusable food wraps, often made from beeswax, fabric, or silicone, are a sustainable alternative to single-use plastic wrap. They can be used multiple times, reducing plastic waste and saving money.

In-Depth Information

How to Use Reusable Food Wraps:

1. **Types of Reusable Food Wraps:**
   - Beeswax wraps
   - Silicone wraps
   - Fabric bowl covers
2. **Steps:**
   - Use the warmth of your hands to mold the wrap around food or containers.
   - Wash with cold water and mild soap after use.
   - Air dry before storing.

Real-Life Example

Example: Emma, a health-conscious foodie, started using beeswax wraps for her lunch and leftovers. She found them easy to use, easy to clean, and perfect for keeping her food fresh.

Implementation in Daily Life

How to Integrate Reusable Wraps:

- **For Snacks and Lunches:** Wrap sandwiches, fruits, and snacks.

- **For Leftovers:** Cover bowls and plates.
- **For Produce:** Wrap cut fruits and vegetables to keep them fresh.

Maintenance Tips:

- Avoid hot water and harsh scrubbing to maintain the integrity of the wraps.
- Replace wraps when they show signs of wear and tear.
- Store wraps in a cool, dry place.

Tip 4: Use a Reusable Water Bottle

Introduction

Why This Tip Matters: Using a reusable water bottle is one of the simplest ways to reduce plastic waste and save money. It helps keep you hydrated throughout the day without relying on single-use plastic bottles.

In-Depth Information

How to Choose a Reusable Water Bottle:

1. **Materials:**
   - Stainless steel
   - Glass
   - BPA-free plastic
2. **Features:**
   - Insulated for temperature control
   - Leak-proof
   - Easy to clean

Real-Life Example

Example: David, a busy executive, switched to a stainless steel water bottle. He enjoyed having cold water all day and was happy to cut down on plastic waste from disposable bottles.

Implementation in Daily Life

How to Use a Reusable Water Bottle:

- **At Work:** Keep the bottle at your desk to encourage regular hydration.
- **At the Gym:** Use the bottle during workouts to stay hydrated.
- **While Traveling:** Carry the bottle with you to avoid buying water on the go.

Maintenance Tips:

- Wash the bottle daily with warm, soapy water.
- Use a bottle brush to clean hard-to-reach areas.
- Regularly check the seal and replace if necessary.

Tip 5: Collect and Use Rainwater for Non-Potable Uses

Introduction

Why This Tip Matters: Collecting rainwater for non-potable uses, such as watering plants or cleaning, is an excellent way to conserve water and reduce utility bills. It's an eco-friendly practice that makes use of a free natural resource.

In-Depth Information

How to Collect Rainwater:

1. **Materials Needed:**
    - Rain barrel or large containers
    - Gutter diverter or downspout
    - Mesh screen to filter debris

2. **Steps:**
    - Install the rain barrel under a downspout.
    - Use the gutter diverter to direct rainwater into the barrel.
    - Cover the barrel with a mesh screen to keep out leaves and insects.
    - Use the collected water for gardening, washing cars, or other non-potable purposes.

Real-Life Example

Example: Jane, an avid gardener, set up a rain barrel in her backyard. She used the collected rainwater to irrigate her plants, significantly reducing her water bill and keeping her garden lush and healthy.

Implementation in Daily Life

How to Use Collected Rainwater:

- **For Gardening:** Water plants, lawns, and flower beds.
- **For Cleaning:** Wash cars, outdoor furniture, and tools.
- **For Pets:** Use the water for pet baths.

Maintenance Tips:

- Clean the rain barrel regularly to prevent algae buildup.
- Check the gutter diverter and downspout for clogs.
- Use a fine mesh screen to filter out small debris.

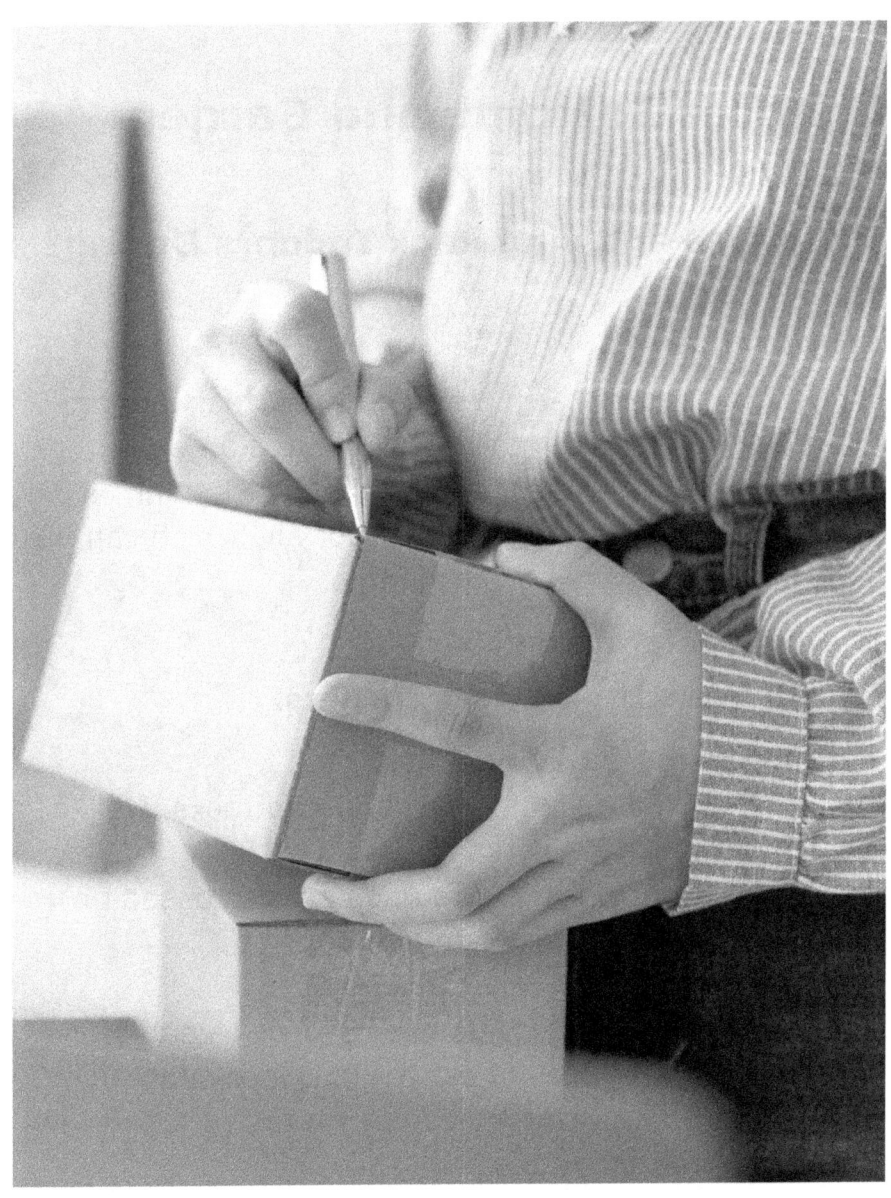

Chapter 3: Home and Garden Hacks

Tip 1: Use a Drying Rack Indoors During Winter

Introduction

Why This Tip Matters: Using a drying rack indoors during winter is an effective way to save on energy costs and reduce wear and tear on your clothing. It also adds moisture to the dry indoor air, which can be beneficial during the colder months.

In-Depth Information

How to Use a Drying Rack Indoors:

1. **Choosing a Drying Rack:**
   - Types: Folding racks, tiered racks, wall-mounted racks.
   - Consider the size and capacity based on your laundry needs.
2. **Steps:**
   - Place the drying rack in a well-ventilated area, ideally near a window or heat source.
   - Spread clothes evenly on the rack to allow for air circulation.
   - Turn clothes occasionally to speed up the drying process.

Real-Life Example

Example: Alex, who lives in a small apartment, started using a drying rack during winter to avoid using the energy-intensive dryer. He noticed a reduction in his electricity bill and found his clothes lasted longer without the high heat of the dryer.

Implementation in Daily Life

How to Make the Most of an Indoor Drying Rack:

- **For Everyday Use:** Dry small loads of laundry regularly to prevent buildup.
- **For Delicates:** Use the rack to dry delicate items that can't go in the dryer.
- **For Extra Humidity:** Use the drying rack in your bedroom or living room to add moisture to the air.

Maintenance Tips:

- Clean the drying rack regularly to prevent mildew.
- Ensure the rack is fully dry before folding and storing.
- Avoid overloading the rack to maintain its shape and functionality.

Tip 2: Bake Multiple Items in the Oven at Once to Save Energy

Introduction

Why This Tip Matters: Baking multiple items in the oven at once maximizes energy efficiency by making the most of the heat generated. This tip not only saves energy but also saves time and money.

In-Depth Information

How to Bake Multiple Items:

1. **Planning:**

- Choose recipes with similar cooking temperatures.
- Arrange baking times so items can go in and come out at the same time.

2. **Steps:**
   - Preheat the oven to the required temperature.
   - Place items on different racks, leaving space for air circulation.
   - Monitor cooking times closely, as having a full oven can sometimes alter baking times.

Real-Life Example

Example: Maria, a busy working mom, started baking her weekly bread, cookies, and a casserole all at once. This saved her both time and energy, allowing her to focus on other tasks while the oven was in use.

Implementation in Daily Life

How to Plan Multi-Item Baking:

- **For Meal Prep:** Bake a week's worth of meals in one session.
- **For Baking:** Make multiple batches of cookies, bread, or pastries at the same time.
- **For Efficiency:** Use all the oven racks to their full potential.

Maintenance Tips:

- Clean the oven regularly to ensure even heat distribution.
- Rotate items between racks if necessary to ensure even baking.

- Use oven-safe thermometers to monitor internal temperatures.

Tip 3: Set Up a Hydroponic Garden

Introduction

Why This Tip Matters: Hydroponic gardening allows you to grow plants without soil, using nutrient-rich water. It's an efficient way to grow vegetables and herbs indoors, saving space and resources.

In-Depth Information

How to Set Up a Hydroponic Garden:

1. **Materials Needed:**
    - Hydroponic system kit or DIY setup
    - Grow lights
    - Nutrient solution
    - Seeds or seedlings
2. **Steps:**
    - Choose a location with sufficient light or install grow lights.
    - Set up the hydroponic system according to instructions.
    - Add the nutrient solution to the water.
    - Plant seeds or place seedlings in the growing medium.
    - Monitor and maintain the system, ensuring plants receive adequate light and nutrients.

Real-Life Example

Example: Tom, a city dweller with limited outdoor space, set up a small hydroponic garden in his apartment. He was able to grow fresh herbs and leafy greens year-round, enjoying the convenience and freshness of home-grown produce.

Implementation in Daily Life

How to Maintain a Hydroponic Garden:

- **For Fresh Produce:** Grow a variety of herbs, lettuce, and other leafy greens.
- **For Space Efficiency:** Utilize vertical hydroponic systems to maximize space.
- **For Easy Maintenance:** Regularly check the nutrient levels and water quality.

Maintenance Tips:

- Clean the system regularly to prevent algae and build-up.
- Replace the nutrient solution as recommended.
- Monitor plant health and adjust lighting and nutrients as needed.

Tip 4: Insulate Your Home with Thick Curtains

Introduction

Why This Tip Matters: Insulating your home with thick curtains helps retain heat during winter and keep rooms cool in summer. This simple tip can significantly reduce energy bills and increase comfort.

In-Depth Information

How to Insulate with Curtains:

1. **Choosing Curtains:**
    - Opt for heavy fabrics like velvet, wool, or thermal-insulated curtains.
    - Ensure curtains are wide and long enough to cover the entire window area.
2. **Steps:**

- Install curtain rods close to the ceiling and extend them beyond the window frame to prevent drafts.
- Close curtains at night during winter to retain heat.
- Open curtains during the day to let sunlight naturally warm the room.
- Reverse this process in summer to keep rooms cool.

Real-Life Example

Example: Grace, a homeowner in a cold climate, installed thermal-insulated curtains in her living room and bedroom. She noticed a significant decrease in her heating bill and a cozier indoor environment.

Implementation in Daily Life

How to Use Curtains for Insulation:

- **For Winter:** Keep curtains closed during cold nights to retain warmth.
- **For Summer:** Close curtains during the hottest part of the day to block out heat.
- **For Energy Savings:** Pair with other insulation methods for maximum efficiency.

Maintenance Tips:

- Wash curtains as recommended to keep them clean and functional.
- Check for wear and tear and replace as needed.
- Use tiebacks to secure curtains when not in use.

Tip 5: Create Draft Stoppers for Doors and Windows

Introduction

Why This Tip Matters: Draft stoppers help block cold air from entering through gaps under doors and windows, improving your home's insulation. They are easy to make and can significantly reduce heating costs.

In-Depth Information

How to Create Draft Stoppers:

1. **Materials Needed:**
   - Fabric (old towels, sheets, or leftover fabric)
   - Scissors
   - Sewing machine or needle and thread
   - Filling (rice, sand, or polyester stuffing)
2. **Steps:**
   - Cut the fabric into a long rectangle, wide enough to cover the gap.
   - Fold the fabric in half lengthwise, with the right sides facing each other.
   - Sew along the long edge and one short edge, leaving one end open.
   - Turn the fabric right side out and fill with the chosen stuffing.
   - Sew the open end closed.

Real-Life Example

Example: James, a DIY enthusiast, made draft stoppers for all the doors in his home using old towels and rice. He noticed a significant reduction in drafts and his home felt warmer without increasing the heating.

Implementation in Daily Life

How to Use Draft Stoppers:

- **For Doors:** Place draft stoppers at the base of exterior doors to block cold air.
- **For Windows:** Use smaller draft stoppers along window sills.
- **For Energy Efficiency:** Combine draft stoppers with other insulation methods for best results.

Maintenance Tips:

- Check draft stoppers regularly for wear and tear.
- Replace filling as needed to maintain effectiveness.
- Wash the fabric covers periodically to keep them clean.

Chapter 4: DIY Projects and Homemade Solutions

Tip 1: Make Your Own Apple Cider Vinegar

Introduction

Why This Tip Matters: Making your own apple cider vinegar (ACV) is a cost-effective way to utilize apple scraps and create a versatile household product. ACV can be used in cooking, cleaning, and even as a health supplement.

In-Depth Information

How to Make Apple Cider Vinegar:

1. **Materials Needed:**
   - Apple scraps (cores and peels)
   - Sugar
   - Water
   - A large glass jar
   - Cheesecloth or coffee filter
   - Rubber band
2. **Steps:**
   - Fill the jar ¾ full with apple scraps.
   - Dissolve 1 tablespoon of sugar in 1 cup of water and pour over the apple scraps until they are fully submerged.
   - Cover the jar with cheesecloth or a coffee filter and secure with a rubber band.
   - Store in a dark, warm place for 3-4 weeks, stirring daily.
   - Strain out the apple scraps and return the liquid to the jar.

- Cover again and let it ferment for another 3-4 weeks, stirring occasionally.
- Taste the vinegar; once it reaches your desired acidity, transfer it to a bottle for storage.

Real-Life Example

Example: Anna, a home cook, started making her own ACV from apple scraps. She used it in recipes, as a natural cleaner, and even as a hair rinse, saving money and reducing waste.

Implementation in Daily Life
How to Use Apple Cider Vinegar:

- **In Cooking:** Use ACV in dressings, marinades, and sauces.
- **For Cleaning:** Mix with water for an all-purpose cleaner.
- **For Health:** Dilute with water and drink for its potential health benefits.

Maintenance Tips:

- Store ACV in a cool, dark place.
- Ensure the jar is clean and dry before making a new batch.
- Use sterilized equipment to avoid contamination.

Tip 2: Turn Vegetable Scraps into Homemade Vegetable Stock Powder

Introduction

Why This Tip Matters: Turning vegetable scraps into homemade vegetable stock powder is a great way to reduce food waste and create a flavorful, cost-effective cooking ingredient.

In-Depth Information

How to Make Vegetable Stock Powder:

1. **Materials Needed:**
   - Vegetable scraps (carrot peels, onion skins, celery leaves, etc.)
   - Dehydrator or oven
   - Blender or food processor
   - Airtight container
2. **Steps:**
   - Collect and wash vegetable scraps.
   - Dehydrate the scraps until completely dry, either using a dehydrator or an oven set at a low temperature.
   - Blend the dried scraps into a fine powder.
   - Store the powder in an airtight container.

Real-Life Example

Example: Rachel, a sustainability enthusiast, used her vegetable scraps to make stock powder. She loved the rich flavor it added to soups and stews, and appreciated the reduction in food waste.

Implementation in Daily Life

How to Use Vegetable Stock Powder:

- **For Soups and Stews:** Add a tablespoon to enhance the flavor.
- **For Seasoning:** Use as a seasoning for vegetables and grains.
- **For Storage:** Store in a cool, dry place for up to six months.

Maintenance Tips:
- Ensure scraps are fully dehydrated to prevent mold.
- Label the container with the date to track freshness.
- Use clean, dry utensils to avoid contamination.

Tip 3: Use Old Coffee Grounds to Clean Greasy Pots

Introduction

Why This Tip Matters: Reusing old coffee grounds to clean greasy pots is a practical way to recycle waste and tackle tough kitchen messes without harsh chemicals.

In-Depth Information

How to Clean with Coffee Grounds:

1. **Materials Needed:**
   - Used coffee grounds
   - Sponge or cloth
2. **Steps:**
   - After brewing coffee, collect the used grounds.
   - Sprinkle the grounds directly onto greasy pots and pans.
   - Scrub with a sponge or cloth in circular motions.
   - Rinse thoroughly with warm water.

Real-Life Example

Example: Mike, an avid coffee drinker, started using his coffee grounds to clean his greasy cookware. He found it effective and appreciated the eco-friendly approach.

Implementation in Daily Life
How to Reuse Coffee Grounds:

- **For Cleaning:** Use as an abrasive cleaner for tough kitchen messes.
- **For Gardening:** Add to compost or use as a fertilizer for plants.
- **For Deodorizing:** Place in the fridge or freezer to neutralize odors.

Maintenance Tips:

- Store used grounds in a dry, airtight container until ready to use.
- Avoid using on surfaces that can stain, like light-colored countertops.
- Dispose of grounds properly to prevent clogging drains.

Tip 4: Create Homemade Bird Feeders
Introduction
Why This Tip Matters: Creating homemade bird feeders is a fun, cost-effective way to attract birds to your yard. It's an excellent use for recyclables and provides essential food for local wildlife.

In-Depth Information
How to Make Homemade Bird Feeders:

1. **Materials Needed:**
    - Empty toilet paper rolls or pine cones
    - Peanut butter or vegetable shortening
    - Birdseed

- String

2. **Steps:**
    - Spread peanut butter or vegetable shortening over the outside of the toilet paper roll or pine cone.
    - Roll in birdseed until fully coated.
    - Tie a string around one end for hanging.
    - Hang the feeder on a tree branch or hook.

Real-Life Example

Example: Sam and his children enjoyed making bird feeders from pine cones and peanut butter. They hung them in the backyard and delighted in watching the birds come to feed.

Implementation in Daily Life

How to Use Homemade Bird Feeders:

- **For Birdwatching:** Place feeders in viewable areas to attract birds.
- **For Educational Purposes:** Teach children about birds and nature.
- **For Garden Health:** Encourage bird visits to help control insects.

Maintenance Tips:

- Refill feeders regularly with fresh birdseed.
- Clean feeders periodically to prevent mold and disease.
- Place feeders away from areas where cats and other predators can reach them.

Tip 5: Use Homemade Herbicides

Introduction

Why This Tip Matters: Homemade herbicides offer a natural, eco-friendly way to manage weeds without harmful chemicals. They are cost-effective and easy to make using common household ingredients.

In-Depth Information

How to Make Homemade Herbicides:

1. **Ingredients Needed:**
   - Vinegar
   - Salt
   - Dish soap
2. **Steps:**
   - Mix 1 gallon of vinegar with 1 cup of salt and 1 tablespoon of dish soap.
   - Pour the mixture into a spray bottle.
   - Apply directly to weeds on a sunny day.

Real-Life Example

Example: Ben, a gardener, switched to using homemade herbicides to control weeds in his garden. He found it effective and appreciated avoiding harmful chemicals.

Implementation in Daily Life

How to Use Homemade Herbicides:

- **For Pathways and Driveways:** Spray on weeds growing in cracks and crevices.
- **For Gardens:** Use carefully to avoid harming desirable plants.

- **For Regular Maintenance:** Apply regularly to prevent weed growth.

Maintenance Tips:

- Store herbicide mixture in a labeled container out of reach of children and pets.
- Reapply as necessary, especially after rain.
- Use protective gloves when handling and applying.

Chapter 5: Thrifty Shopping and Resource Management

Tip 1: Shop at Thrift Stores

Introduction

Why This Tip Matters: Shopping at thrift stores is a budget-friendly way to find quality items at a fraction of the cost. It supports sustainability by giving secondhand goods a new life and reduces waste.

In-Depth Information

How to Shop at Thrift Stores:

1. **Tips for Finding Great Deals:**
    - Visit regularly, as inventory changes frequently.
    - Go early for the best selection.
    - Look for sales and discount days.
2. **Steps:**
    - Make a list of what you need to stay focused.
    - Inspect items carefully for quality and condition.
    - Try on clothing and test electronics before purchasing.

Real-Life Example

Example: Laura, a fashion enthusiast, discovered thrift shopping as a way to find unique, affordable clothing. She enjoyed the thrill of the hunt and the satisfaction of saving money.

Implementation in Daily Life

How to Make the Most of Thrift Shopping:

- **For Clothing:** Find stylish, gently used clothes at a fraction of the retail price.
- **For Home Goods:** Discover unique decor items and kitchenware.
- **For Books and Media:** Stock up on books, movies, and music for less.

Maintenance Tips:

- Wash and sanitize items after purchasing.
- Check for store return policies in case of issues.
- Donate unused items back to the thrift store to continue the cycle.

Tip 2: Host a Neighborhood Book Exchange

Introduction

Why This Tip Matters: Hosting a neighborhood book exchange promotes reading, saves money on buying new books, and fosters a sense of community. It's a simple way to share and discover new literature.

In-Depth Information

How to Host a Book Exchange:

1. **Planning the Event:**
    - Choose a location (e.g., community center, park, or your home).
    - Set a date and time.
    - Promote the event through flyers, social media, and word of mouth.
2. **Steps:**

- Ask participants to bring books they'd like to exchange.
- Set up tables or shelves for displaying books.
- Create a system for trading books (e.g., one-for-one exchange).

Real-Life Example

Example: Emily organized a book exchange in her neighborhood. It became a monthly event where neighbors gathered to trade books and discuss their favorite reads, building a stronger community bond.

Implementation in Daily Life

How to Encourage Participation:

- **For Families:** Promote as a family-friendly event to encourage participation.
- **For Book Clubs:** Combine with book club meetings for added engagement.
- **For Community Building:** Use as an opportunity to meet new neighbors and make friends.

Maintenance Tips:

- Keep track of popular genres and requested books for future events.
- Ensure a variety of books are available to appeal to different interests.
- Collect leftover books and donate them to libraries or charities.

Tip 3: Dehydrate Fruits for Homemade Snacks

Introduction

Why This Tip Matters: Dehydrating fruits at home is a cost-effective way to create healthy, preservative-free snacks. It's an excellent method to preserve seasonal fruits and reduce food waste.

In-Depth Information

How to Dehydrate Fruits:

1. **Materials Needed:**
   - Fresh fruits
   - Dehydrator or oven
   - Lemon juice (optional, to prevent browning)
2. **Steps:**
   - Wash and slice the fruits evenly.
   - Dip slices in lemon juice if desired.
   - Arrange slices on dehydrator trays or baking sheets.
   - Dehydrate at 135°F (57°C) until completely dry (6-12 hours in a dehydrator, longer in an oven).

Real-Life Example

Example: Sarah, a health-conscious mom, started dehydrating fruits for her kids' snacks. They loved the tasty treats, and she appreciated knowing exactly what was in their food.

Implementation in Daily Life

How to Use Dehydrated Fruits:

- **For Snacks:** Pack in lunchboxes or take on-the-go.
- **For Baking:** Use in recipes for muffins, breads, and granola.
- **For Storage:** Store in airtight containers for long-term use.

Maintenance Tips:

- Store dehydrated fruits in a cool, dark place.
- Check for moisture content regularly to prevent mold.
- Label containers with the date to track freshness.

Tip 4: Make Handmade Gifts

Introduction

Why This Tip Matters: Making handmade gifts is a thoughtful, personal way to celebrate special occasions without spending a lot of money. It allows you to create unique, customized presents that recipients will cherish.

In-Depth Information

How to Make Handmade Gifts:

1. **Ideas for Handmade Gifts:**
   - Knitted or crocheted items (scarves, hats, blankets)
   - Homemade candles or soaps
   - Personalized photo albums or scrapbooks
2. **Steps:**
   - Choose a gift idea based on the recipient's interests.
   - Gather the necessary materials.
   - Follow tutorials or guides to create the gift.

- Personalize with special touches (e.g., monograms, favorite colors).

Real-Life Example

Example: Lisa, an amateur crafter, made homemade candles as holiday gifts. She personalized each one with scents and colors she knew her friends and family would love, making the gifts extra special.

Implementation in Daily Life

How to Plan for Handmade Gifts:

- **For Holidays:** Start early to ensure you have enough time to complete projects.
- **For Birthdays:** Create a list of upcoming birthdays and plan gifts in advance.
- **For Special Occasions:** Customize gifts for weddings, anniversaries, and other celebrations.

Maintenance Tips:

- Keep crafting supplies organized and readily accessible.
- Follow safety guidelines when working with tools and materials.
- Practice new techniques before starting a gift project.

Tip 5: Turn Vegetable Peels into Homemade Vegetable Chips

Introduction

Why This Tip Matters: Turning vegetable peels into homemade chips is a tasty way to reduce food waste. It's a simple, healthy snack option that makes use of every part of your vegetables.

In-Depth Information

How to Make Vegetable Chips:

1. **Materials Needed:**
    - Vegetable peels (potatoes, carrots, beets, etc.)
    - Olive oil or cooking spray
    - Salt and seasonings
    - Baking sheet
2. **Steps:**
    - Preheat the oven to 400°F (200°C).
    - Wash and dry the vegetable peels thoroughly.
    - Toss peels with a small amount of olive oil or cooking spray.
    - Spread peels in a single layer on a baking sheet.
    - Sprinkle with salt and desired seasonings.
    - Bake for 10-15 minutes, turning halfway through, until crispy.

Real-Life Example

Example: Jane, a home cook, started saving her vegetable peels and turning them into chips. Her family loved the crunchy, flavorful snack, and she felt good about reducing kitchen waste.

Implementation in Daily Life

How to Enjoy Vegetable Chips:

- **For Snacks:** Enjoy as a healthy alternative to store-bought chips.
- **For Toppings:** Use as a crunchy topping for soups and salads.

- **For Parties:** Serve as a unique, homemade appetizer.

Maintenance Tips:

- Store chips in an airtight container to maintain freshness.
- Experiment with different seasonings to find your favorite flavors.
- Make small batches to ensure the chips stay crisp.

Conclusion

Recap of Key Points

As we reach the end of this book, let's take a moment to reflect on the key points we've covered. From upcycling and repurposing household items to embracing eco-friendly practices and making homemade solutions, we've explored various ways to live a frugal yet fulfilling life. The tips provided are designed to help you save money, reduce waste, and enhance your overall well-being.

Encouragement to Adopt Frugal and Productive Habits

Adopting frugal living and productive habits may seem challenging at first, but remember that every small step counts. Start with one or two tips that resonate with you and gradually incorporate more into your daily routine. The journey to a more frugal and sustainable lifestyle is ongoing, and the benefits you reap will grow over time. By making mindful choices, you can achieve financial stability, environmental stewardship, and a sense of personal satisfaction.

Teaser for Volume 2

Stay tuned for Volume 2 of this series, where we will delve deeper into additional tips and strategies for frugal living and productivity. We will explore more advanced techniques, including financial planning, DIY home improvements, and creative ways to repurpose everyday items. Volume 2 will provide further inspiration and practical advice to help you continue your journey towards a more frugal and rewarding life.

Invitation for Reader Feedback

Your feedback is invaluable to us. We would love to hear about your experiences with the tips and strategies presented in this book. Did you find them helpful? Are there any areas you'd like us to explore further in future volumes? Please share your thoughts and suggestions, as they will help us improve and tailor our content to better meet your needs. Feel free to reach out via email or through our website.

Appendix

Additional Resources

Books:

- "The Complete Tightwad Gazette" by Amy Dacyczyn: A comprehensive guide to frugal living with tips on saving money in all areas of life.
- "Your Money or Your Life" by Vicki Robin and Joe Dominguez: A transformative approach to managing your finances and achieving financial independence.
- "The Zero-Waste Home" by Bea Johnson: A practical guide to reducing waste and living sustainably.

Websites:

- **Budget Bytes:** budgetbytes.com: Affordable and delicious recipes for budget-conscious cooks.
- **The Frugal Girl:** thefrugalgirl.com: Tips and stories about frugal living, DIY projects, and mindful spending.
- **Mr. Money Mustache:** mrmoneymustache.com: A blog focused on financial independence and early retirement through frugal living and smart investing.

Tools:

- **Mint:** mint.com: A free budgeting tool that helps you track spending, create budgets, and manage your finances.

- **YNAB (You Need A Budget):** ynab.com: A powerful budgeting tool that teaches you how to gain control of your money and build a financial cushion.
- **Evernote:** evernote.com: An organizational tool to help you manage tasks, save ideas, and keep track of important information.

Worksheets and Templates

Budget Templates:

- Monthly Budget Planner: A simple template to help you track your income, expenses, and savings each month.
- Yearly Financial Goals: A worksheet to set and track your financial goals for the year, including saving targets and debt repayment plans.

DIY Project Plans:

- Step-by-Step Instructions: Detailed plans for DIY projects mentioned in this book, including homemade cleaning cloths, draft stoppers, and braided rugs.
- Materials Checklist: A comprehensive list of materials needed for various DIY projects to help you stay organized and prepared.

Frugality Trackers:

- Savings Tracker: A visual tracker to monitor your savings progress and keep you motivated.
- Waste Reduction Log: A worksheet to record your waste reduction efforts and track the impact of your eco-friendly practices.

"Frugal Living and Productivity Tips: Volume 1"

Discover the Secrets to a More Frugal, Productive, and Fulfilling Life!

Are you looking to save money, reduce waste, and boost your productivity without sacrificing quality or comfort? "Frugal Living and Productivity Tips: Volume 1" is your ultimate guide to achieving financial freedom and a sustainable lifestyle. Packed with 25 practical tips, this book will help you transform your daily habits, make smarter choices, and unlock the full potential of frugal living.

Inside, you'll learn how to:

- Repurpose household items into valuable resources
- Adopt eco-friendly practices to save money and the environment
- Boost your productivity with simple, effective strategies
- Create DIY projects that enhance your home and life

Real-Life Examples and Step-by-Step Instructions: Each tip comes with detailed explanations, real-life success stories, and easy-to-follow steps to ensure you can start implementing these strategies right away. Whether you're a young professional, a busy parent, a college student, or a retiree, this book is designed to meet you where you are and help you achieve your goals.

Join the Frugal Living Movement: Embrace a lifestyle of sustainability, creativity, and financial freedom. With "Frugal Living and Productivity Tips: Volume 1," you'll discover that living well on less isn't just possible—it's incredibly rewarding.

Notes:

www.ingramcontent.com/pod-product-compliance
Lightning Source LLC
Chambersburg PA
CBHW071958210526
45479CB00003B/981